Smithsonian

LITTLE EXPLORER

FISH

A 4D BOOK

by Melissa Higgins

CAPSTONE PRESS
a capstone imprint

Download the Capstone 4D app!

- Ask an adult to download the Capstone 4D app.
- Scan the cover and stars inside the book for additional content.

When you scan a spread, you'll find fun extra stuff to go with this book! You can also find these things on the web at www.capstone4D.com using the password: fish.26448

Little Explorer is published by Capstone Press,
1710 Roe Crest Drive, North Mankato, Minnesota 56003
www.mycapstone.com

The name of the Smithsonian Institution and the sunburst logo are registered trademarks of the Smithsonian Institution. For more information, please visit www.si.edu.

Library of Congress Cataloging-in-Publication Data
Names: Higgins, Melissa, 1953– author.
Title: Fish : a 4D book / by Melissa Higgins.
Description: North Mankato, Minnesota : an imprint of Pebble, [2019] |Series: Smithsonian little explorer. Little zoologist | Audience: Age 4–8.
Identifiers: LCCN 2018004118 (print) | LCCN 2018009137 (ebook) | ISBN 9781543526561 (eBook PDF) | ISBN 9781543526448 (hardcover) | ISBN 9781543526509 (paperback)
Subjects: LCSH: Fishes—Juvenile literature.
Classification: LCC QL617.2 (ebook) | LCC QL617.2 .H54 2019 (print) | DDC 597—dc23
LC record available at https://lccn.loc.gov/2018004118

Editorial Credits

Michelle Hasselius, editor; Kazuko Collins, designer;
Sveta Zhurkin, media researcher;
Kris Wilfahrt, production specialist

Our very special thanks to XX. Capstone would also like to thank Kealy Gordon, Product Development Manager, and the following at Smithsonian Enterprises: Ellen Nanney, Licensing Manager; Brigid Ferraro, Vice President, Education and Consumer Products; Carol LeBlanc, Senior Vice President, Education and Consumer Products; and Christopher A. Liedel, President.

Image Credits
Alamy: blickwinkel, 29 (top and bottom right), Mark Conlin, 13, 29; AP Photo: The Winchester Star/Ginger Perry, 5 (bottom); Dreamstime: Lukas Blazek, 19, 29; Getty Images: Jeff Rotman, 18; iStockphoto: olegkozyrev, 5 (top); Newscom: Photoshot/NHPA/Nigel Downer, 28, Photoshot/NHPA/Paulo de Oliveira, 8–9, 29, Polaris/Evelyn Hockstein, 4; Shutterstock: Ammit Jack, 6, Anneke Swanepoel, 21 (top), Arunee Rodloy, 27 (bottom), Grigorii Pisotsckii, 24, Licvin, 11, Longchalerm Rungruang, 20, 29, Mirko Rosenau, 2, 23, Santi Rodriguez, 1, Serban Bogdan, 21 (bottom), somdul, 26, Vadym Zaitsev, 12, Vladimir Wrangel, 10, 16–17, 29, Volodymyr Burdiak, 25, 29, You Touch Pix of EuToch, 22–23, 29; Smithsonian's National Zoo: Abby Wood, cover, 7, 27 (top), 29, Courtney Smith, 15, 29

Printed and bound in the United States.
PA021

TABLE OF CONTENTS

THE NATION'S ZOO 4

ARAPAIMA 6

BANDED LEPORINUS 8

BLACK PACU 10

CHANNEL CATFISH 12

ELECTRIC EEL 14

FLAGTAIL CHARACIN 16

FRESHWATER STINGRAY 18

JAPANESE KOI 20

PLECOSTOMUS 22

RED-BELLIED PIRANHA 24

SILVER AROWANA 26

TWIG CATFISH 28

GLOSSARY 30

CRITICAL THINKING QUESTIONS 31

READ MORE 31

INTERNET SITES 31

INDEX 32

The Smithsonian's National Zoo opened in 1889. It is located in Washington, D.C. Curators, animal keepers, and veterinarians take care of the 1,800 animals living at the Zoo. These animals represent 300 species. About 76 species are fish.

The Smithsonian Conservation Biology Institute (SCBI) is also part of the Smithsonian's National Zoo. It was built in 1974 and is in Front Royal, Virginia. Here, scientists study endangered species. Their goal is to keep these animals from dying out.

A scientist at SCBI held a newborn black-footed ferret in 2014.

Smithsonian
National Zoological Park

About 2 million people visit the Zoo each year. They come from all over the world.

The Smithsonian Conservation Biology Institute is usually closed to the public. It opens its doors one day a year. On Conservation Discovery Day, guests can take tours and talk to scientists.

ARAPAIMA

The arapaima are some of the biggest fish in the Amazon River. They can weigh up to 400 pounds (181 kilograms). The arapaima can be 10 feet (3 meters) in length. They live in shallow water and breathe air. They can live for an hour and a half out of the water.

Arapaima make their home in the Amazonia exhibit at the Zoo. They eat fish, squid, shrimp, and fruit. Like many fish at the Zoo, the arapaima are also fed a special gel. To make the gel, keepers mix food in a blender with gelatin. These gels are very healthy for the fish.

The arapaima suck in food like vacuums. They eat other fish and plants. Birds and small mammals are also on the menu.

Their tongues are covered with bony teeth. The teeth help break up food.

The banded leporinus are hard to miss. These zebra-striped fish have bold black and yellow stripes along their bodies. They are almost 10 inches (25 centimeters) long.

Banded leporinus eat plants, fruits, and leaves. At the Zoo's Amazonia exhibit, they are also fed leafy vegetables and gel.

These sleek fish zip through fast-moving streams in the Amazon River basin. Banded leporinus often swim together in schools. When predators are nearby, these fish hide in holes along the bottom of the river.

When these fish hatch, they have five black stripes. They get more stripes as they grow.

BLACK PACU

The black pacu look like fierce piranhas. One difference between the two fish is their teeth. Unlike the piranha's sharp teeth, the black pacu have square teeth. They look like human molars.

The black pacu have lived at the Amazonia exhibit for more than 25 years.

This black pacu can grow up to 3 feet (1 m) long. They can weigh more than 65 pounds (29 kg).

The fish live in the Amazon River. They eat mostly fruits, nuts, and plants. At the Zoo's Amazonia exhibit, keepers feed them fruit, sweet potatoes, and worms.

CHANNEL CATFISH

Channel catfish live on the bottoms of ponds and rivers all over North America. They have gray-blue sides and black backs. Most grow to about 1 foot (0.3 m) long. They weigh about 3 pounds (1 kg). But they can grow larger. One of the biggest channel catfish ever caught was 58 pounds (26 kg).

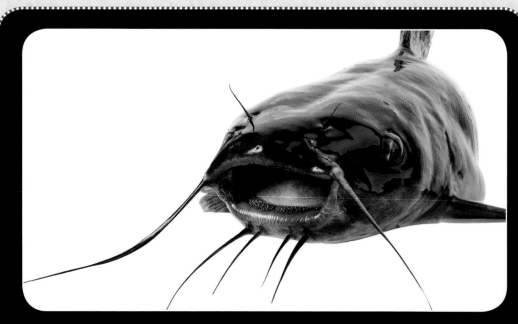

These catfish have four pairs of barbels on their mouths. The barbels help the fish smell and taste food—even in muddy water.

Channel catfish eat whatever they can find. This might be algae, plants, or insects. At the Zoo these fish also eat food pellets. The pellets are dry cubes made up of healthy fish food.

At the Zoo the channel catfish are found in the pond at the Kid's Farm. The Kid's Farm is also home to cows, alpacas, miniature donkeys, goats, chickens, and Ossabaw island hogs.

ELECTRIC EEL

The electric eel has a shocking surprise. Three organs in its body can make electricity—the main electric organ, the Hunter's organ, and the Sach's organ. Electric eels can release 600 to 800 volts of electricity. This can stun prey and scare away predators. They also use small electric charges to communicate with each other and swim through water.

These snake-like fish can grow up to 8 feet (2.4 m) long. In the wild they live in slow-moving water in the Amazon and Orinoco Rivers. They eat fish, frogs, crabs, shrimp, and other invertebrates. At the Amazonia exhibit, keepers feed electric eels fish, shrimp, and worms. Keepers must wear rubber gloves so they don't get shocked.

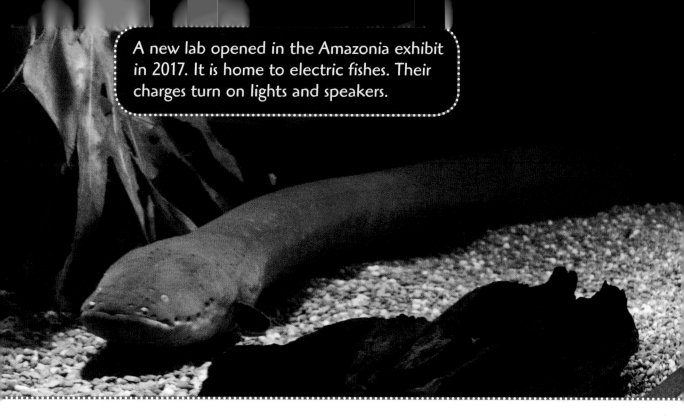

A new lab opened in the Amazonia exhibit in 2017. It is home to electric fishes. Their charges turn on lights and speakers.

ZAP!

The electric eel can pack a big shock. Compare the electric eel to other power sources.

AA battery: 1.5 volts

car battery: 12.6 volts

house outlet: 120 volts

subway electric rail: 625 volts

electric eel: 600–800 volts

FLAGTAIL CHARACIN

The flagtail characin are freshwater fish. Their yellow-orange fins and tails stand out from their silver bodies. These fish are about 14 inches (35.6 cm) long.

In the wild, most flagtail characin live in the central and western parts of the Amazon River. Their home at the Zoo is at the Amazonia exhibit. They eat tiny plants. Keepers also feed them gel.

The school of flagtail characins are some of the oldest fish at the Zoo. They are more than 24 years old.

Freshwater stingrays live in the Amazon River. Like other stingrays, they have round bodies with long tails. Their tails are tipped with one or two spines. These spines hold venom. One strike from a stingray's tail can be very painful. But stingrays only use their spines to protect themselves.

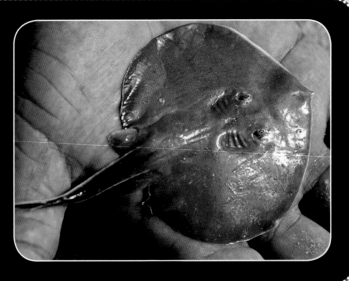

Most fish lay eggs. Stingrays give birth to live young, called pups. Females have two to six pups each year.

Freshwater stingrays eat worms and fish. They also use their strong jaws to eat crabs, shrimp, clams, and mussels. At the Zoo's Amazonia exhibit, keepers feed them shrimp and worms.

JAPANESE KOI

Japanese koi are originally from Asia. Now they live all over the world. These bright fish come in many colors. Koi can grow up to 3 feet (0.9 m) long.

Koi means "carp" in Japanese.

A number of Japanese koi live at the Kid's Farm. Keepers feed them floating pellets. Insects, algae, and plants are on the menu too.

Japanese koi can live a long time. The oldest lived for 230 years.

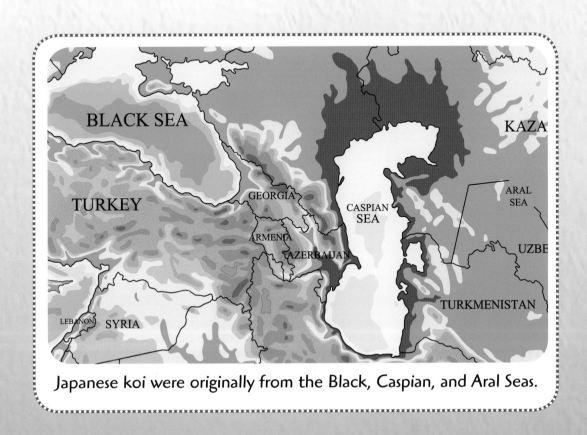

Japanese koi were originally from the Black, Caspian, and Aral Seas.

PLECOSTOMUS

The plecostomus are also known as suckermouth catfish. They live in fast-flowing streams in the Amazon River basin. These catfish build nests by digging in mud. They also live in caves made by driftwood or rocks. The plecostomus can grow 20 inches (51 cm) long.

The plecostomus are nicknamed the "wood-eating catfish." This is because they're the underwater termite of the Amazon.

Their mouths are located underneath their heads. This helps them scrape and suck up algae. The plecostomus also eat plants and fish. At the Zoo's Amazonia exhibit, keepers feed them plants and gel.

Male plecostomus guard and take care of their eggs. They fan and clean the eggs until they are ready to hatch.

Bony plates cover the plecostomus' body. The back plates are thicker than the rest.

Red-bellied piranhas are eating machines. Strong muscles are connected to their jaws. Their razor-sharp teeth bite down hard onto prey. These piranha swim in schools. Staying together keeps them safe from large predators.

The red-bellied piranha have thick lips that make their sharp teeth hard to see.

Piranhas mainly eat the tails off of bigger fish. They sneak up behind larger fish, rush in, eat part of the tail, and swim away. They also eat small fish, insects, figs, and other fruit. At the Zoo's Amazonia exhibit, keepers feed them smelt, herring, shrimp, earthworms, and gels.

SILVER AROWANA

The silver arowana lives in the Amazon River basin. It is more than 39 inches (99 cm) long.

The silver arowana's mouth opens at the top of its head. It eats spiders and insects on the water's surface. It jumps out of the water to eat large insects, snails, snakes, and small birds. Keepers at the Amazonia exhibit feed the silver arowana shrimp and fish.

young silver arowanas

Males carry their eggs and young inside their mouths. They do this until the young fish can survive on their own. This can take two months.

It is easy to see how twig catfish got their name—they looks like twigs. These small catfish live throughout the Amazon River basin. They are also found in other rivers in South America. The twig catfish can grow to about 6 inches (15 cm) long. Bony plates protect them from predators.

Twig catfish are one of the only fish species that eat wood. Their spoon-shaped teeth scrape at wood. At the Amazonia exhibit, they are also fed zucchini, cucumbers, plants, and gel.

underneath a twig catfish

These fish can easily hide among dead leaves and sticks.

HOW DEEP?

Fish live in different depths of water in rivers and ponds.

SHALLOW

arapaima

silver arowana

MIDDLE

black pacu

flagtail characin

red-bellied piranha

DEEP

banded leporinus

channel catfish

electric eel

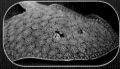
freshwater stingray

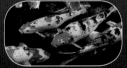
Japanese koi

plecostomus

twig catfish

GLOSSARY

algae—small plants without roots or stems that grow in water

barbel—a feeler around the mouths of some fish

basin—an area of land that drains into a river

curator—a person in charge of an exhibit

endangered—at risk of dying out

exhibit—a display that shows something to the public

fin—a body part that fish use to swim in water

freshwater—water that does not have salt; most ponds, rivers, lakes, and streams are freshwater

gelatin—a clear substance used to make jelly, desserts, and glue

mammal—a warm-blooded animal that breathes air and has hair or fur; female mammals feed milk to their young

molars—wide teeth that people use to chew food; molars are in the back of the mouth

organ—a part of the body that does a certain job; the heart, lungs, and kidneys are organs

predator—an animal that hunts other animals for food

prey—an animal hunted by another animal for food

school—a large number of the same kind of fish; schools of fish swim and eat together

species—a group of plants or animals that share common a common ancestor and common characteristics

spine—a hard, sharp, pointed growth

stream—a small body of flowing water; streams join other streams to form a river

venom—a poison that is injected or stabbed into the body

veterinarian—a doctor who treats sick or injured animals; veterinarians help animals stay healthy

volt—a unit for measuring electricity

CRITICAL THINKING QUESTIONS

1. How many animal species live at the Smithsonian's National Zoo? How many of these species are fish?

2. Black pacu look like piranhas. How are they different? Use the text to help you with your answer.

3. The flagtail characin have yellow-orange fins. What are fins?

READ MORE

Amstutz, Lisa J. *Fish.* My First Animal Kingdom Encyclopedia. North Mankato, Minn.: Capstone Press. 2017.

Bennett, Elizabeth. *Curious About Fishes.* New York: Grosset & Dunlap, 2015.

Lawrence, Ellen. *Arapaima.* Apex Predators of the Amazon Rain Forest. New York: Bearport Publishing. 2017.

INTERNET SITES

Use FactHound to find Internet sites related to this book.

Visit www.facthound.com

Just type in 9781543526448 and go.

 Check out projects, games and lots more at
www.capstonekids.com

INDEX

Amazon River, 6, 11, 14, 17, 18
Amazon River basin, 9, 22, 26, 28

babies, 9, 18, 27

color, 8, 9, 10, 16, 20, 24, 26, 27

diet, 6, 8, 11, 13, 14, 17, 19, 23, 25, 27, 28

eggs, 18, 23, 27
exhibits,
    Amazonia, 6, 8, 10, 11, 14, 15, 17, 19, 23, 25, 27, 28
    Kid's Farm, 13, 21

Front Royal, Virginia, 4

Orinoco River, 14

schools, 9, 17, 24
size, 6, 8, 11, 12, 14, 16, 20, 22, 26, 28
Smithsonian Conservation Biology Institute, 4, 5

Washington, D.C., 4

Zoo jobs,
    curators, 4
    keepers, 4, 11, 14, 17, 21, 23, 25, 27
    veterinarians, 4